PERICLES

THE LEADER WHO GREW UP IN WARS

BIOGRAPHY FOR KIDS 9-12

CHILDREN'S BIOGRAPHY BOOKS

BABY PROFESSOR

EDUCATION KIDS

Speedy Publishing LLC

40 E. Main St. #1156

Newark, DE 19711

www.speedypublishing.com

Copyright 2017

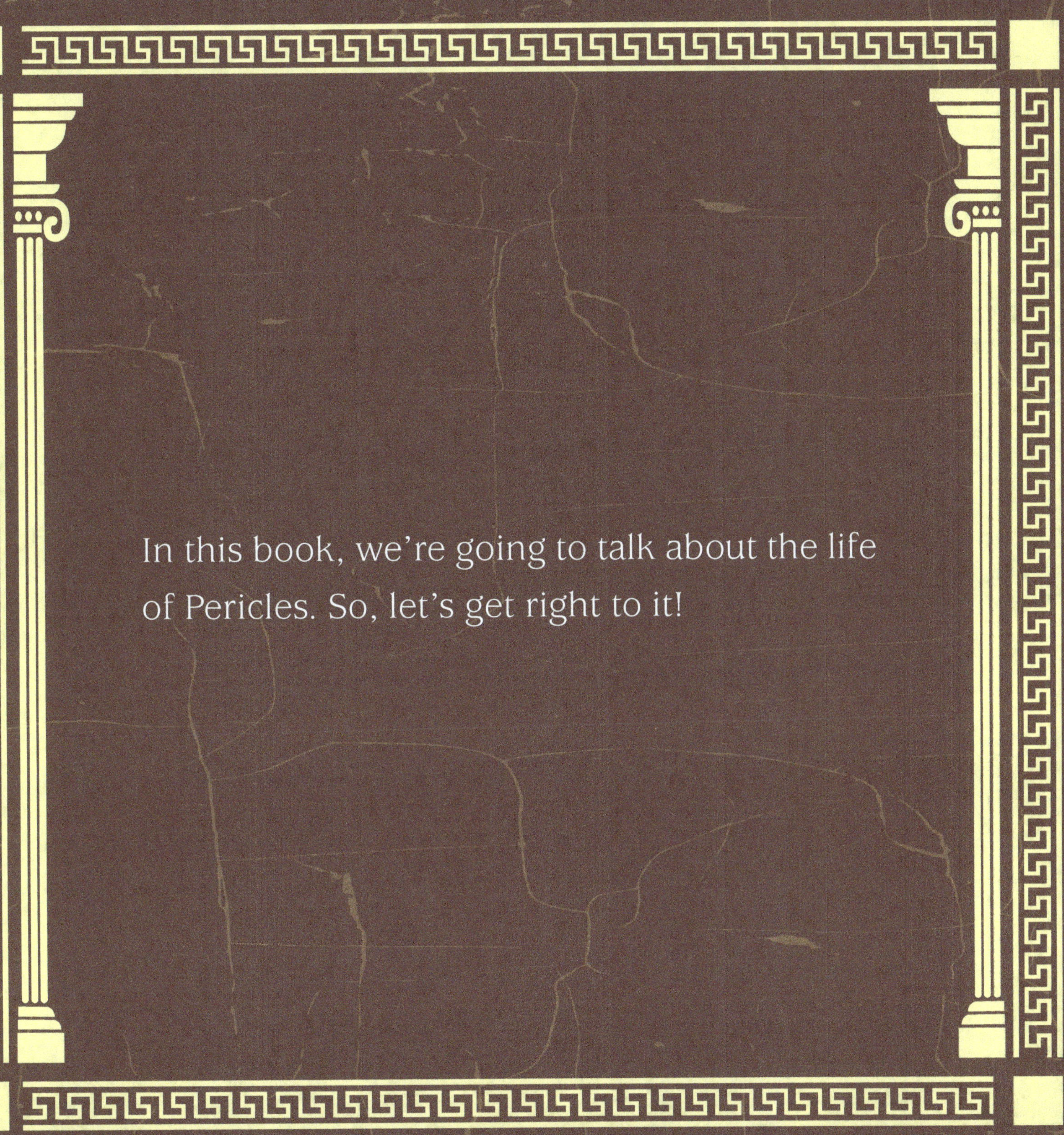

In this book, we're going to talk about the life of Pericles. So, let's get right to it!

WHO WAS PERICLES?

Pericles was a Greek statesman who was born in 495 B.C. and passed away in 429 B.C. His name means "surrounded by glory" and Pericles became famous in his lifetime. He was a great speaker as well as a patron of the arts. As a patron, he helped artists, writers, and philosophers achieve their most masterful works by encouraging their freedom of expression.

He was also a general and a politician. He became well known for his achievements and his beliefs, which influenced Greece and eventually had an effect on all of Western civilization. He was so important to Greek society that the Greek historian Thucydides proclaimed that he was the "first citizen" of the democracy of Athens.

GENERAL PERICLES

THE AGE OF PERICLES

Pericles had a wide circle of friends and associates. These talented people became the center of society in Athens. In fact, he was so influential that this "Golden Age" of Athens has been called the "Age of Pericles." The city became a cultural center and a thrilling place for artists to live and work. During this time, the great Greek playwrights, such as Sophocles and Euripedes as well as Aeschylus and Aristophanes, created the beginnings of what we know today as the theater.

Hippocrates, who was the father of modern medicine, healed the sick during this era and we know him today for the Hippocratic oath. Masterful sculptors like Myron and Phidias created classic statues that breathed life into marble. The great philosophers Protagoras and Zeno of Elea were close friends of Pericles. Socrates also taught philosophy during this time. Pericles was the first statesman to give credence to the importance of the study of philosophy.

The construction of the architectural wonders of the Parthenon and other temples on the Acropolis happened during this era as well. After Pericles passed away, this golden age of the city-state of Athens passed away as well.

Pericles was born into a wealthy family of nobles in 495 B.C.

CHILDHOOD AND EARLY LIFE

His father's name was Xanthippus. He was a military hero who had fought in the Persian War. Pericles's mother was named Agariste of Sicyon. The well-known statesman and democratic reformer Cleisthenes was her uncle and they were both members of the influential Alcmaeonidae family.

Wartime influenced Pericles's childhood. When he was three years of age, Athens was attacked by the empire of Persia. However, the Athenians prevailed when they were victorious at the Battle of Marathon. A decade later, Athens was once again attacked by the Persians and the Athenian citizens fled while the Persians destroyed much of the city.

BURIAL MOUND OF THE 192 ATHENIAN
FALLEN AT THE BATTLE OF MARATHON

BATTLE OF SALAMIS

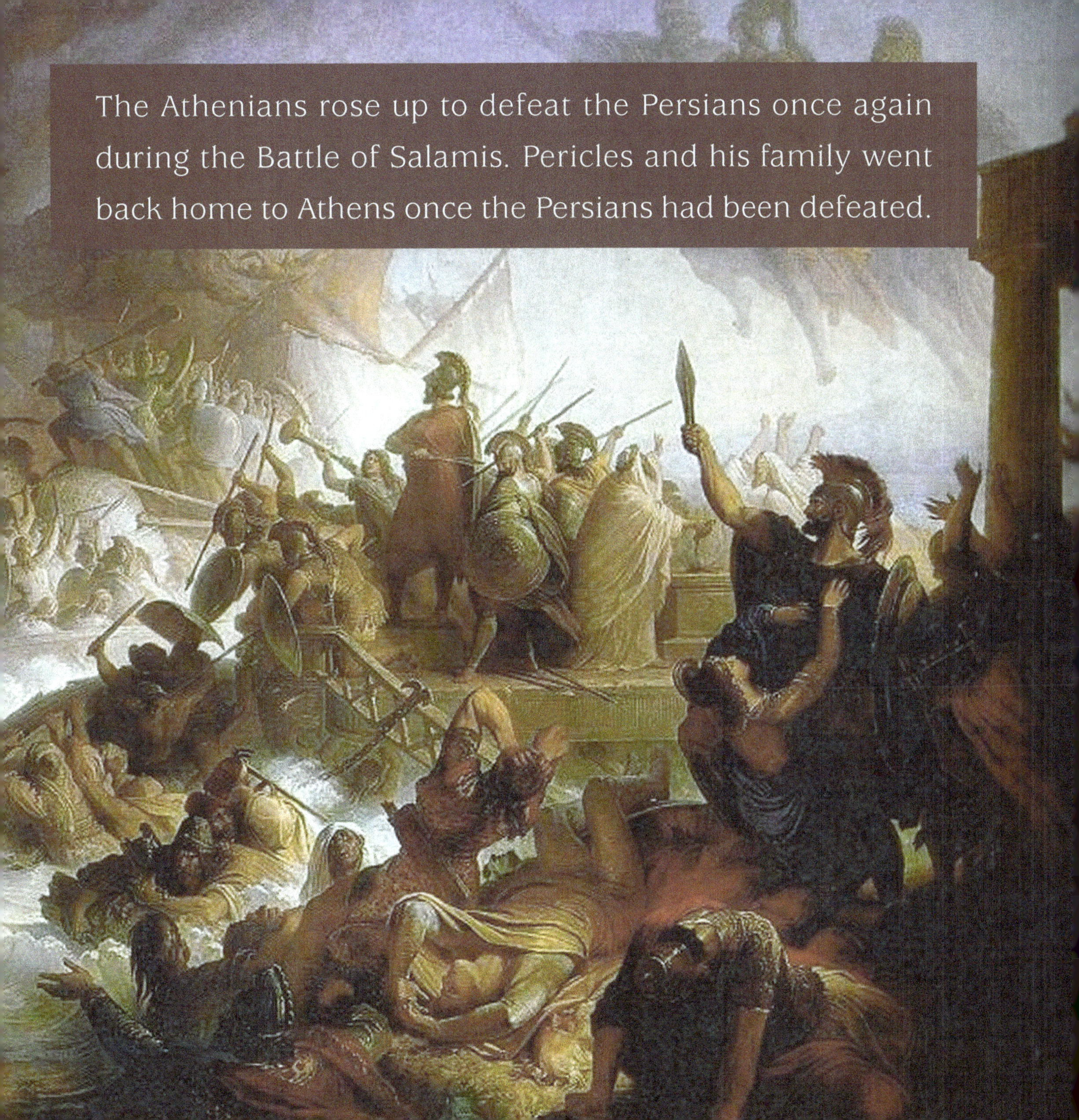

The Athenians rose up to defeat the Persians once again during the Battle of Salamis. Pericles and his family went back home to Athens once the Persians had been defeated.

Because his family was wealthy, Pericles had the luxury of spending much of his youth studying Greek philosophy and music from the leading masters in these fields. As a youngster, he was very introverted and didn't enjoy going out in public, but this behavior changed as he got older. He always had a very calm demeanor and this ability to think clearly helped him as a military strategist in later life.

By the time Pericles was 17 years old, he had inherited a large amount of money. He began to fund great works of art. One of the first major investments he made was a play written by Aeschylus called "The Persians," which was performed in 472 B.C. The play was the story of the Battle of Salamis. The performance was also meant to support the politician Themistocles, who was the popular candidate, instead of Cimon, who was an aristocrat. It was a way for Pericles to express his political views. The play was very successful and today it's believed to be the text of the oldest surviving play. It brought Pericles into the public eye and he became popular in society.

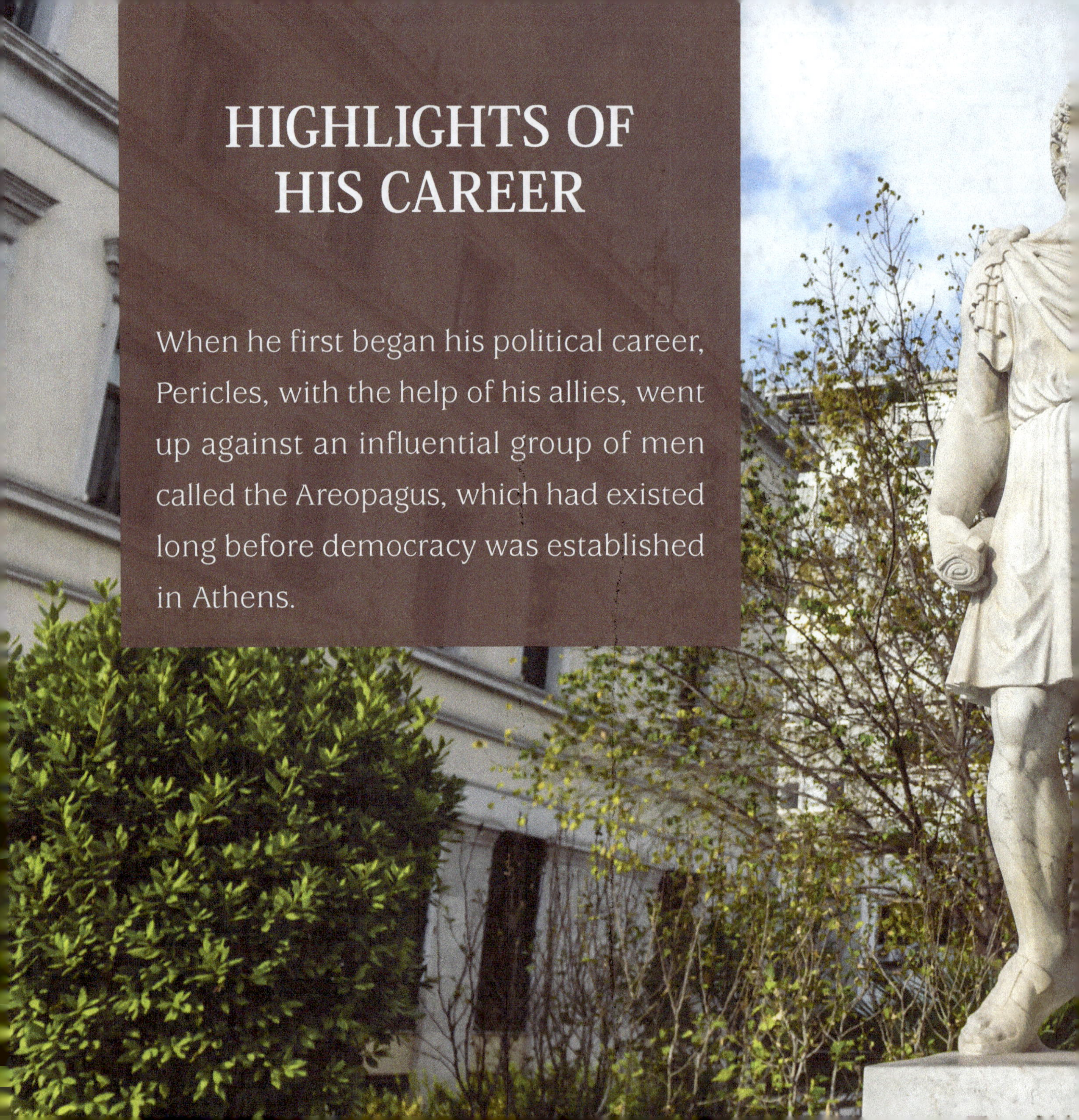

HIGHLIGHTS OF
HIS CAREER

When he first began his political career,
Pericles, with the help of his allies, went
up against an influential group of men
called the Areopagus, which had existed
long before democracy was established
in Athens.

Pericles succeeded in decreasing the influence of this traditional group and thereby strengthened "power by the people" in Athens. He became important in politics as a result.

ODEON OF PERICLES IN ATHENS

In 461 B.C., he also succeeded in getting the aristocrat Cimon banished for betraying the city. Due to this action, Pericles became the head of the democratic party in Athens.

Pericles was forty-one years old when he went forth with his first military campaign in 454 B.C during the First Peloponnesian War. He and his troops attacked Sicyon as well as Acarnania. He also tried to conquer Oeniadea, but wasn't successful. He established two new Athenian colonies, one in Thrace and another on the coast of the Black Sea.

THRACE, GREECE

RUINS OF DELPHI NEAR PHOCIS, GREECE

During the military conflict with Sparta called the Second Sacred War, Pericles led the attack against Delphi and reinstated the region of Phocis so that it had rights to the oracle of Delphi. The oracle was a powerful individual in Athenian society who gave advice and foretold the future.

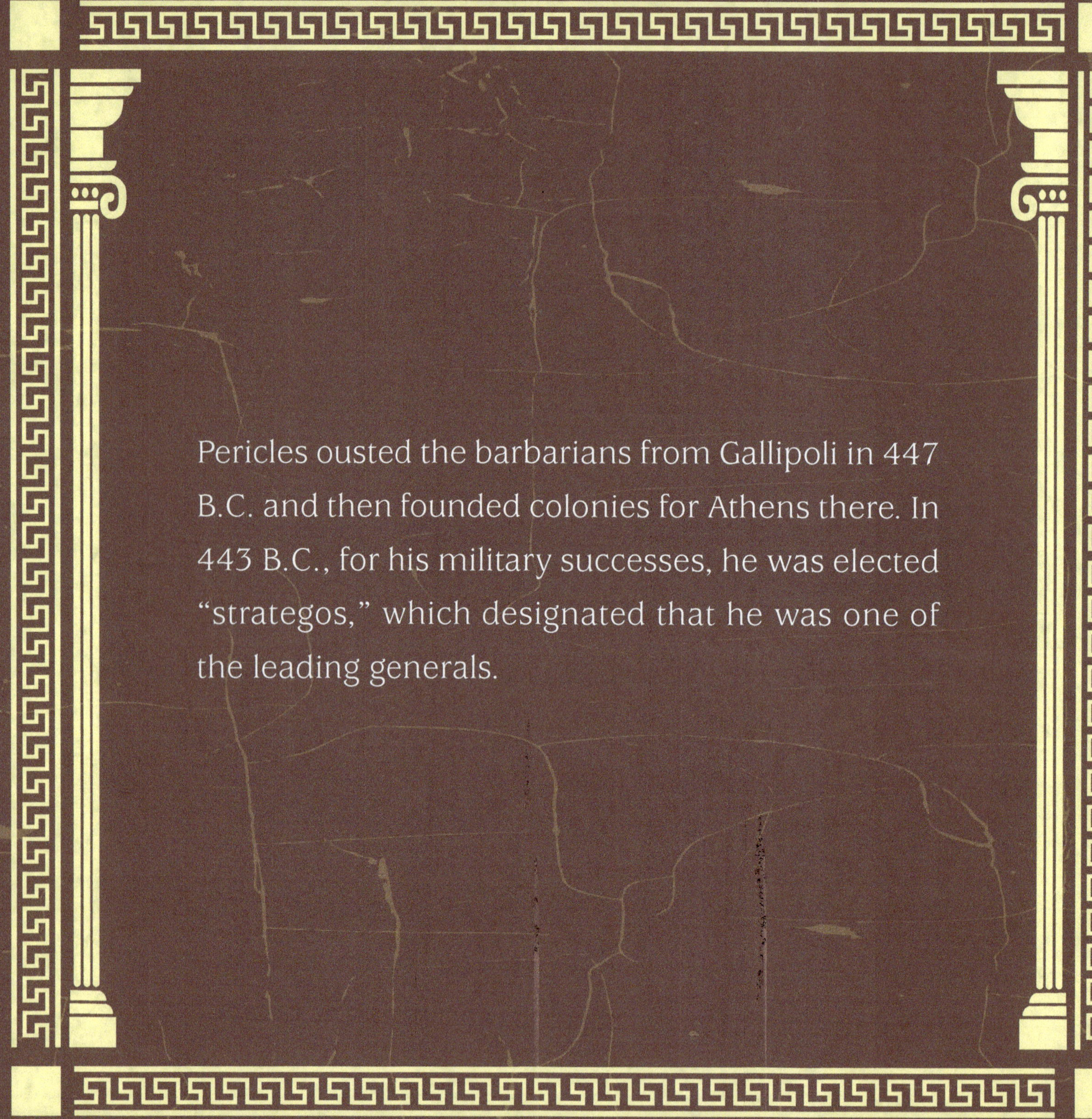

Pericles ousted the barbarians from Gallipoli in 447 B.C. and then founded colonies for Athens there. In 443 B.C., for his military successes, he was elected "strategos," which designated that he was one of the leading generals.

ODEON OF PERICLES

CORINTH, GREECE

As the city-state of Athens became more wealthy and powerful under Pericles's direction, Sparta became concerned. In 431 B.C., the Peloponnesian War between the two rivals broke out when there was a conflict between Athens and Corinth, which was a supporter of Sparta. Archidamus II, who was the king of Sparta, attacked Attica, a city close to Athens.

The Spartan armies were superior to the Athenian armies so Pericles used a strategy. He had the citizens of Attica flee to Athens so the Spartan armies had no one to fight. Then, he used the superior Athenian navy attack the allies of Sparta by sea. Although this strategy was expensive to implement, it worked at the start.

ATTICA, GREECE

A FAMOUS ORATION

After the Peloponnesian War started, Pericles gave a speech, which was later called the Funeral Oration. This famous speech was dedicated to the Athenian soldiers who had died in battle. It paid homage to the ideals of democracy that the city-state of Athens and Pericles stood for. The text of Pericles's speech still exists and has helped historians understand that period of Grecian history.

THE PLAGUE COMES TO ATHENS

Throughout the wars with Sparta, it had been Pericles's strategy to fight them on the sea instead of on land where they had superior armies. The Athenians had built long walls to the closest seaport so they could get supplies. During the Peloponnesian War they gathered in the city to stay protected from the Spartans. However, a plague occurred and thousands died. Eventually, in 429 B.C., their great leader Pericles contracted the plague and passed away. Athens eventually lost the war and never regained the glory they had under the Age of Pericles.

DEATH OF PERICLES

FAMOUS BUILDING PROJECTS

In addition to his many other achievements, Pericles is known for his successful building projects.

From the years 449 to 431 B.C, Pericles
invested in several of the famous buildings
in Athens, especially those located on the
Acropolis, including:

The Parthenon, a beautiful temple to the goddess
Athena, which is still partially standing today

The Athena Nike, a temple
in honor of Athena Nike, the
goddess of victory

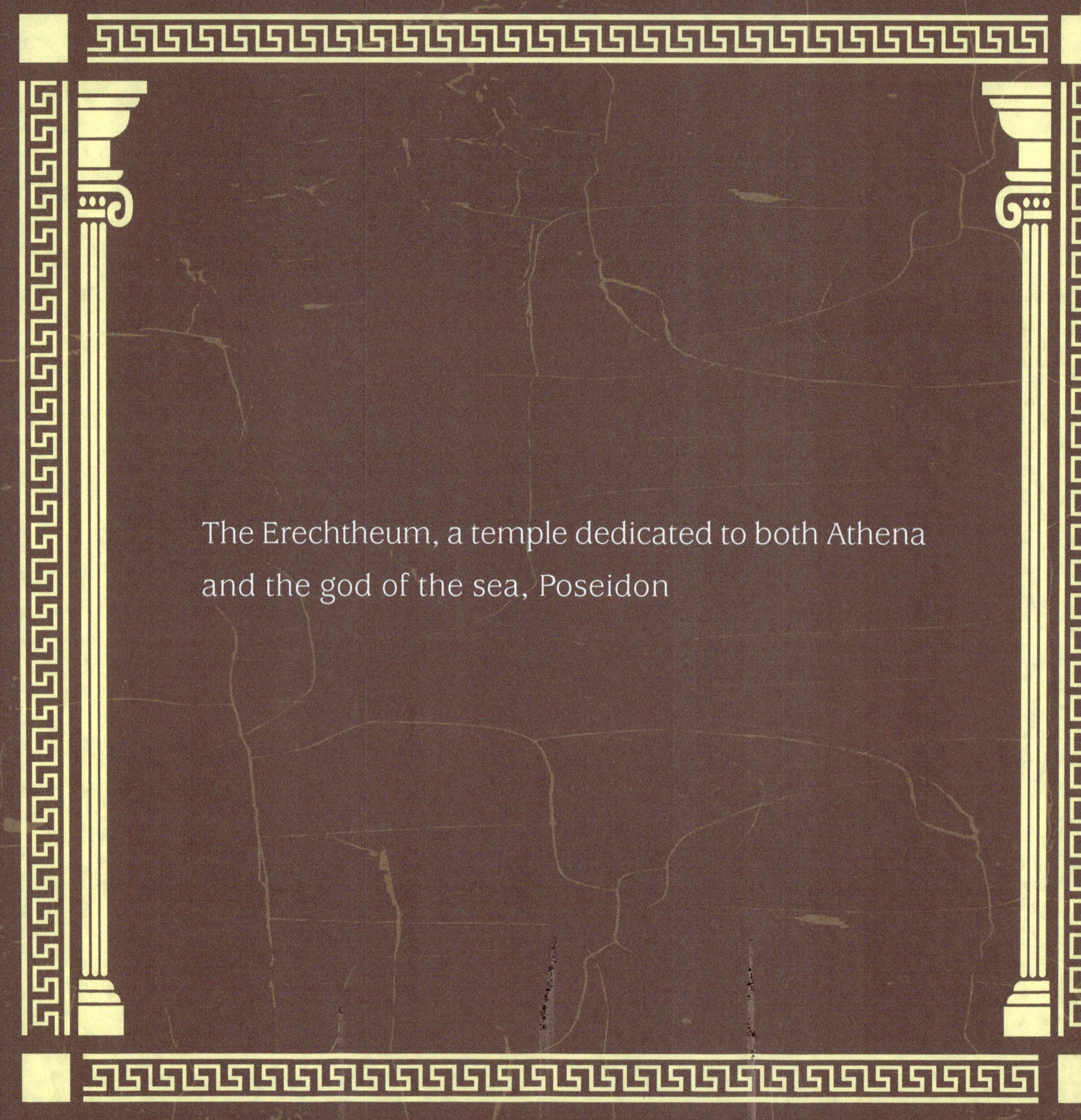
The Erechtheum, a temple dedicated to both Athena
and the god of the sea, Poseidon

ERECHTHEUM

FASCINATING FACTS
ABOUT PERICLES

Pericles was known to have a very elongated skull.
His enemies and critics called him "squill-head"
after the bulb of a sea onion plant.

Before Pericles was born, his mother had a dream about a lion. Dreams about lions have been linked to men with powerful influence. The mother of Alexander the Great also had a dream about a lion before his birth.

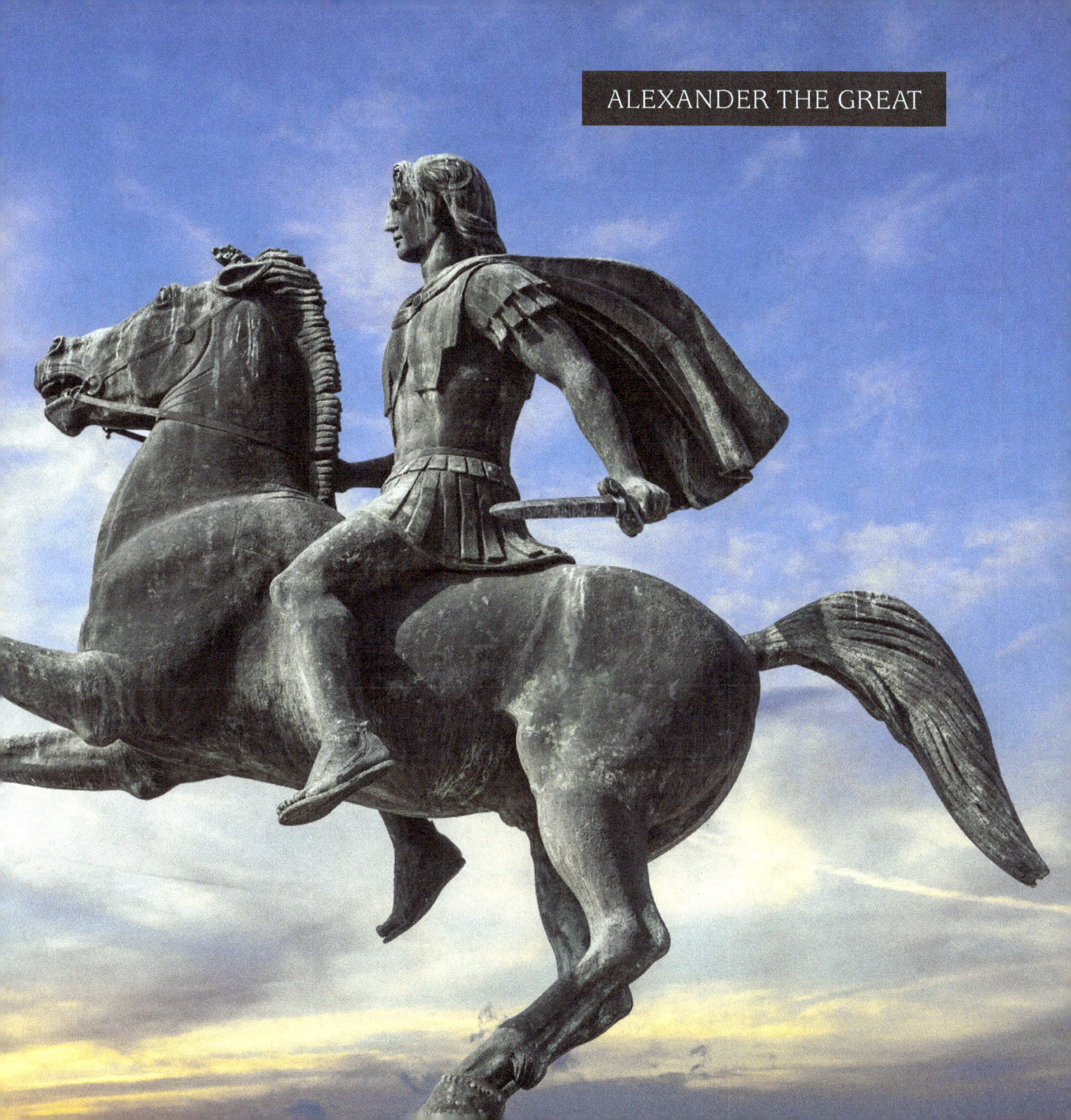
ALEXANDER THE GREAT

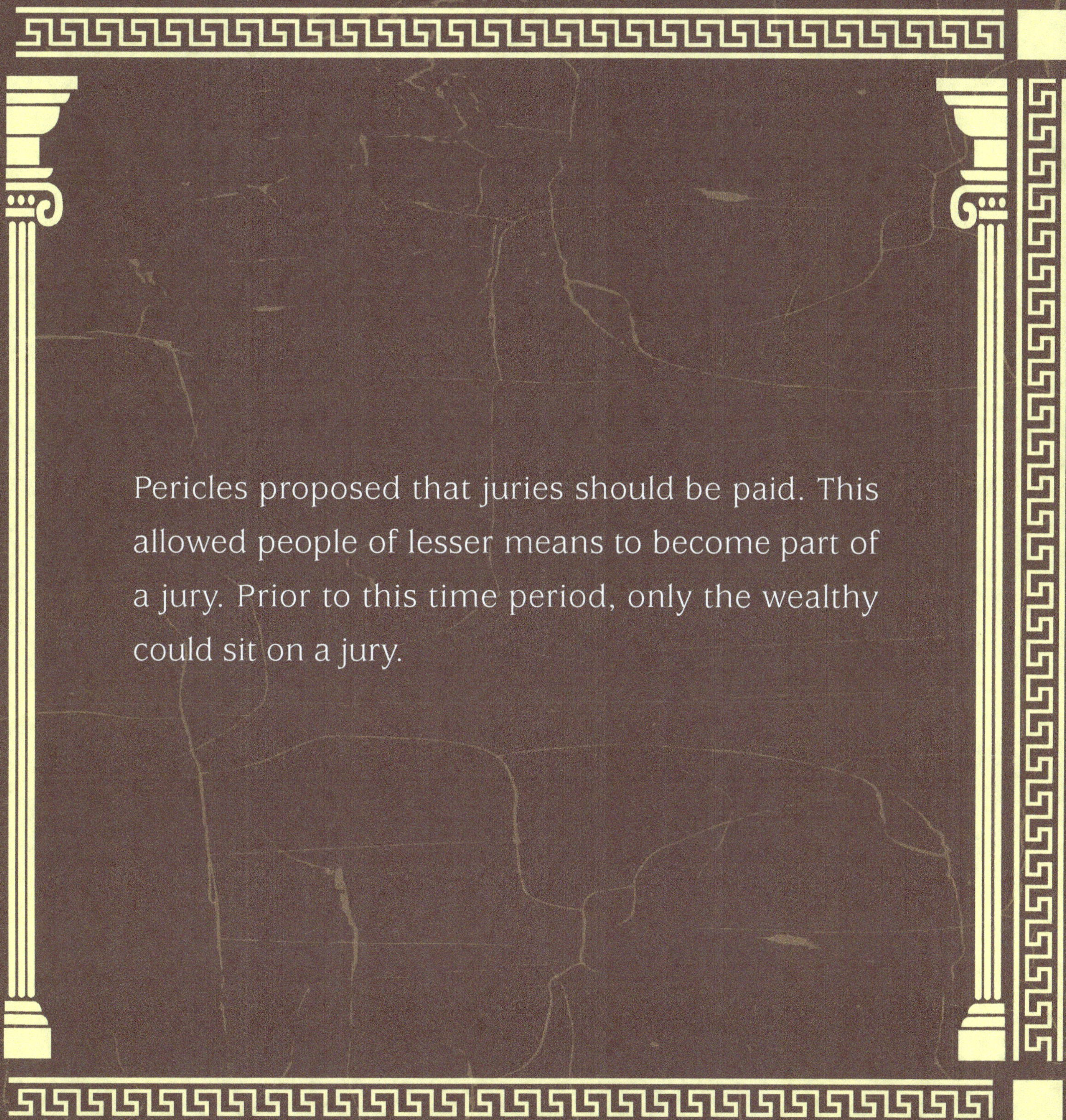

Pericles proposed that juries should be paid. This allowed people of lesser means to become part of a jury. Prior to this time period, only the wealthy could sit on a jury.

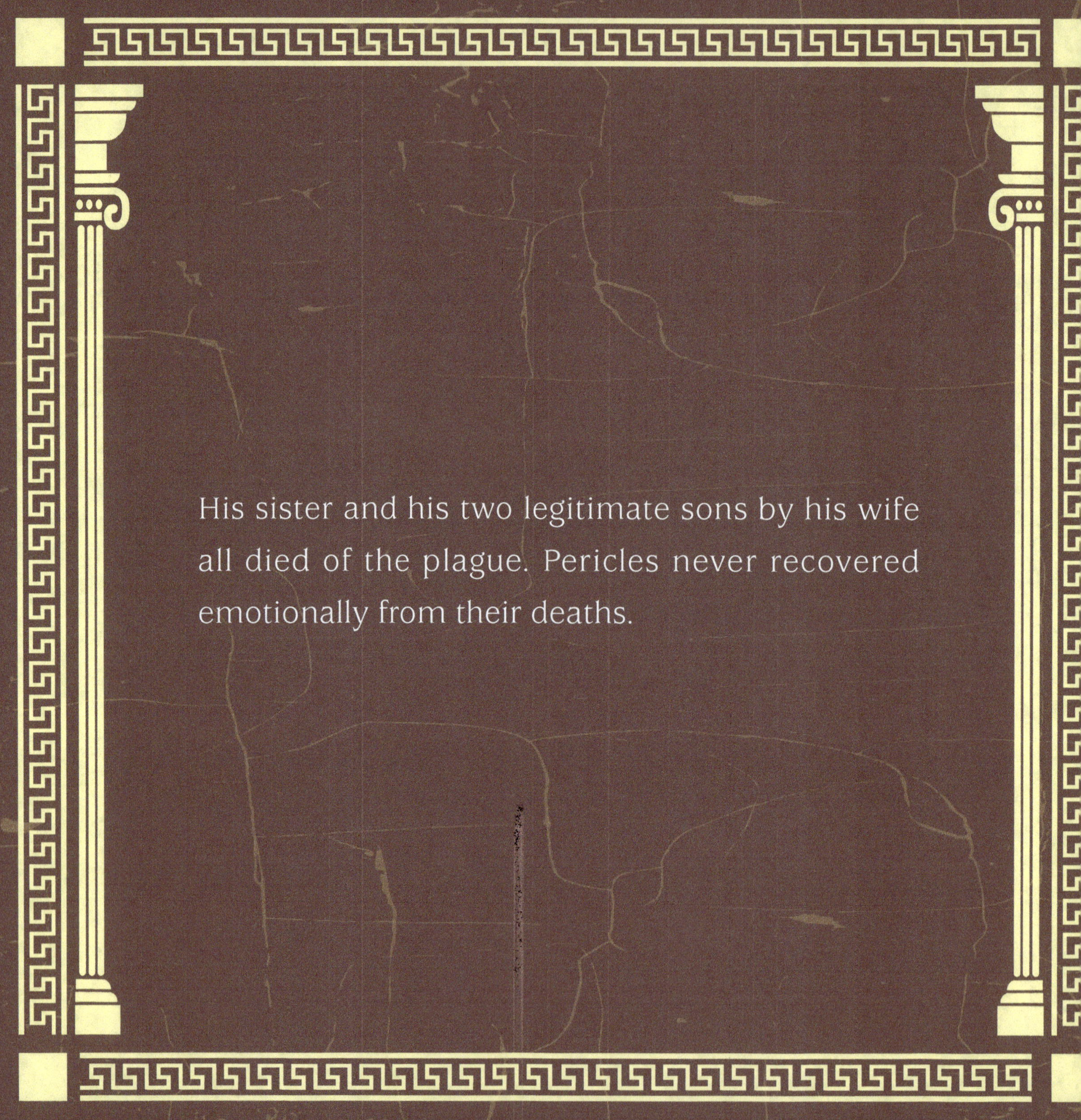

His sister and his two legitimate sons by his wife all died of the plague. Pericles never recovered emotionally from their deaths.

ASPASIA

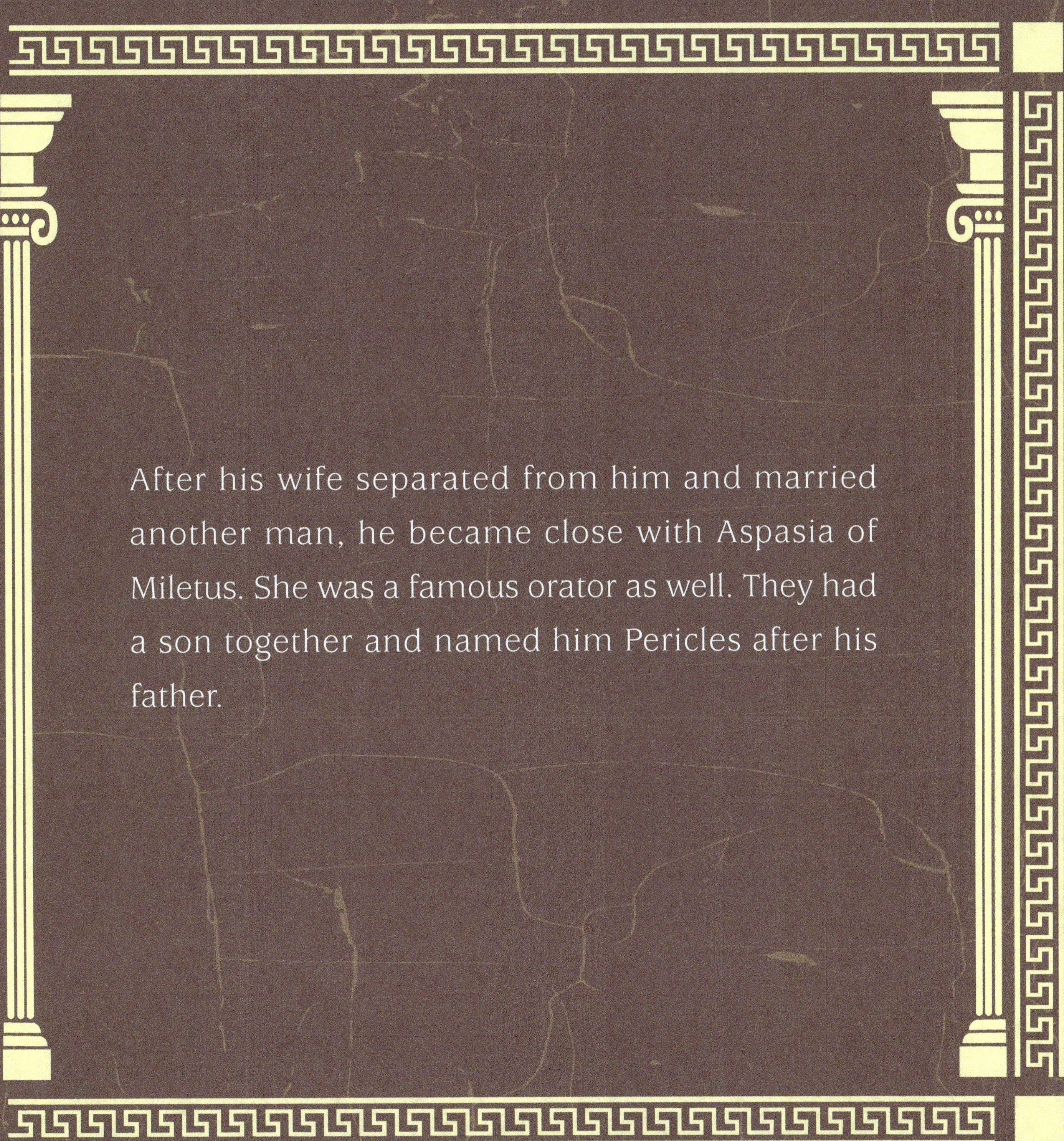

After his wife separated from him and married another man, he became close with Aspasia of Miletus. She was a famous orator as well. They had a son together and named him Pericles after his father.

PERICLES' INFLUENCE

Born into a wealthy noble family, Pericles was a Greek statesman, orator, and general. He lived from 495 B.C. until 429 B.C. He was an influential speaker and military man as well as a patron of the arts.

ΠΕΡΙΚΛΗΣ

Because of his influence, the city-state of Athens had a golden age of culture, art, architecture, democratic rule, and military power.

Awesome! Now that you've learned about the life of Pericles, you may want to read about Ancient Greece and how it affected our world today in the Baby Professor book The Effects of Ancient Greece in Modern Times – History Lessons 3rd Grade.

Visit
BABY PROFESSOR
EDUCATION KIDS
www.BabyProfessorBooks.com
to download Free Baby Professor eBooks
and view our catalog of new and exciting
Children's Books